THE AD\
OF ML
RUNNING

A guide to mindfulness for runners
seeking greater performance and
enjoyment.

Dr Gemma Applegarth

Dedicated to our beautiful minds. They give us thought, judgement, love, and the joy of the present moment. It is an adventure to live life with you.

With grateful thanks to all who have supported me. To the running club who encouraged me to face the hills and the mindfulness coaches who passed on wisdom. I am thankful to have shared the journey with you all.

Extra special thanks to my wife and beautiful son. Thank you for always being yourselves, just as you are.

CONTENTS

CHAPTER 1

THE ADVENTURE BEGINS

It was a chilly winter morning. The wind was biting through my clothes. I could feel the thickness of the mud that caked my legs. Looking down I could see I was covered. My trainers were barely recognisable, pale blue turned to a dark brown. The icy chill of water seeped through onto my toes.

Cross country running really is the most fun for me. There is no way I could be this cold, dirty and covered in mud, without feeling alive and invigorated. I had found my pure joy. The same joy I had as a child running for the pure enjoyment of movement. My mind wandered back over the journey I had been through.

As a child I had been encouraged to take part in sports by marathon running parents. I was never pushed to perform, simply to take part and it worked for me. I had loved walking my dog deep into the country, playing tennis and football with friends, skateboarding and roller-skating. I even had several years learning martial arts.

Later in life I took up running with my friends. We were quite sporadic in our commitment. The occasional charity 5K run or Sunday morning plod around the fields. We got a bit carried away one year and decided to have a go at a half marathon. I underestimated the challenge but survived, hobbling over the finish line. We even signed up to do it again and I was thrilled to take 30 minutes off my time. I was fit, I was healthy.

Then something happened to bring it all to an end. Put simply, my mind got in the way. I realised I wasn't naturally talented at any of these things, I had fears of coming last or looking daft. It became easier to let life take over, and life really did. I went to university and enjoyed the pleasures of being a student, including the daytime drinking and fast food. Soon I had piled on the pounds and was reaching the end of my degree. I took on a doctorate and a full-time graduate job. The next few years passed by in a blur of work, commuting, long hours in the library and nutrition which came from a vending machine.

I woke up at 35. I was having palpitations from far too many energy drinks. I somehow had become clinically obese, and some health checks revealed underlying health conditions possibly caused by lifestyle. I couldn't ignore that it was time to make a change.

A few months of procrastinating later, I finally found myself stood in a field, watching an invigorated instructor demonstrate warm up exercises to a cohort of couch to 5K hopefuls. As I approached the course I was overwhelmed with negative thoughts. In mindfulness we often discuss the difference between the emotional mind and the meditative mind.

My emotional mind kicked in with volume and persistence. It was like machine gun fire in my mind, one thought after another, each one accompanied by an urge to stay in the car or head home. The easiest thing would have been to simply give up. It would have taken me away from the anxiety and given me a more peaceful evening. Here is an example of what my emotional mind was saying.

Emotional Mind Say it out loud, at speed and repeat to get a sense of what it felt like to hear. Notice if any of this feels familiar to you.

"What's the point? You are now too overweight for this. You won't be able to do it. You should just give up. You will be last. They say it's a beginner's course but what if people are better than you. Go home. Have a nice evening on the sofa. It's too cold for this and you are too tired from work".

Around this time, I was undertaking training in teaching mindfulness skills. Meditation was something I had been using to help with wellbeing and exam stress for a few years and I had been delighted to be offered a place on a teaching course that would allow me to pass these skills on to others.

I decided to put my mindfulness skills to the test. When situations came up at work or in life that made me this anxious, I would use mindfulness to put a little space between me and my thoughts. I wondered if this was any different. My emotional mind wasn't allowing me to experience how running might feel, instead it was adding a layer of suffering to my overwhelmed emotions by telling me how it would be. How could it possibly know? I hadn't even got out of the car yet.

The thoughts that popped into my mind weren't new, they had been a part of the story I had told myself for many years. It seemed I would experience these kinds of negative thoughts whether I gave them permission to be there or not.

The meditative mind works differently from the emotional mind. The big difference is the way the meditative mind responds to these thoughts. Instead of trying to push them away or give in to the urge to turn on the car engine and enjoying my evening on the sofa with a takeaway, it simply acknowledges the thoughts and the urge to react.

As I checked in with the thoughts and emotions that were present, I found myself accepting their presence. Many of the thoughts I noticed were predicting the future, telling me what my experience of the course would be. Others reminded me of times when I had found running hard, or hadn't enjoyed being cold, or felt stupid in front of others.

It's amazing this ability the human mind has, to live simultaneously in the past, present, and future all at once. Taking my time, I took a single mindful breath. I acknowledged the thoughts. I even thanked my mind for trying to give me the easy option of giving up. I gently moved myself back into the present through the feeling of my feet connecting with the ground beneath my trainers.

I began to turn down the volume on these thoughts, to step away from their power. Of course, they were still there but I recognised my urge to get back in the car and go straight home was simply a thought.

The space between myself and these thoughts allowed me to join the group. It turned out to be a good move that saw me joining the running club and enjoying the sport again.

That was not the end of the machine gun fire of thoughts. Each time there was a new challenge, a half marathon or joining the cross-country team, the emotional mind made an appearance.

My first winter as a club member was full of buzz and excitement around the cross-country season. Each year the club connected with several other clubs in the area and took it in turn to put on an event. Friendly rivalry between clubs took centre stage as there were points to be earned both for winning performances and mass participation. I knew I would love cross country. I had always loved rural running, being away from the roads and noise. I knew I would love the challenge of the natural landscape and would be invigorated by the chance of ending up face first in giant puddles. Yet the emotional mind fired up once more.

Emotional Mind (say it out loud, at speed and repeat to get a sense of what it felt like to hear, notice if anything is familiar to you).

"You will make a fool of yourself, why bother? You will be last. You can't take part if you're not super-fast. It's all the fast runners that are in the league. You will let the team down. You are better off staying home. You could have a lay in."

Alongside the predictions of the future, the machine gun highlighted memories of school cross country runs, of humiliation that never really happened except in my hormonal teenage mind. The thoughts gave me the urge to let go of the chance to run in favour of Sunday mornings in bed. Once again, I leant on my ongoing meditation practise. I used it to help me notice and explore these thoughts, to accept their presence and to make a choice to join in anyway.

Since then, there have been endless moments where mindfulness has served me well with running. It's not all in the preparation for running either. Mindful running which is the art of bringing full attention to my run has had endless benefits for me. Helping me overcome the thoughts that get in my way before I tackle a big hill and the urge to stay in bed rather than make it to Parkrun.

Mindfulness has allowed me to simply enjoy the process of running. The feeling of strength in my legs as I take a step, the freezing wind on my skin while inside I feel warm. Even the unbelievable feeling of being out early in the morning, just me and the natural world with all its sounds and wonder.

The competitive side of me also benefitted. As I became a regular runner, I became focussed on personal bests. It became important to me to see progress. I was thrilled each time there was a milestone like a longer distance or a new personal best time. Mindfulness gave me the chance to notice when my mind got in the way. It gave me the opportunity to step away from the power of these thoughts and to develop deeper concentration while I was running. I stopped running with music and focussed on really being present with my body and the run.

As I developed mindfulness skills, I was also able to use these to help me work on my positive mindset before an event, to be my own pep talk and to use visualisation to help me develop the self-belief needed.

As I used mindfulness to support both my performance in running and my enjoyment of my active life, I became interested in finding out more about how mindfulness and sports could help others. What I found was an emerging field of Mindful Sports Performance Enhancement (MSPE). I found psychologists studying the impact of giving athletes mindfulness training across a range of sports with promising initial results. Even better, there was a place for mindfulness in supporting all levels of athletes. From the competitive runner with records on their mind to those of us who love to make an appearance at Parkrun once a week and follow it up with a slice of cake.

This book is the result of years of researching mindfulness for sports and practicing mindfulness every day, both for my wellbeing and to enhance my performance and enjoyment of running. The following pages will give you a sense of what mindfulness is, how mindfulness can be applied to running, and give you all you need to start your own mindful running practise.

Your mindful running practise is going to be your teacher. Over time, taking part in the activities in the book can support you to develop an ability to stand back from whatever gets in your way, whether that's negative thoughts, lack of motivation, or emotional blocks that stop you reaching your potential.

CHAPTER 2

WHAT IS MINDFULNESS?

Mindfulness is everywhere. Recent years have seen an explosion in the availability of mindfulness courses, apps, and books. Meditation is now being recommended by doctors, psychologists, wellbeing practitioners and even teachers to help us with a variety of concerns.

A short search of the internet will reveal mindfulness being used for depression, anxiety, wellbeing, stress management, overeating, parenting, sports, and many other concerns. So, what is all this mindfulness buzz about?

Mindfulness refers to the awareness that emerges for us when we learn how to pay attention to the present in a way that is deliberate, on purpose and allows us to simply observe our experience of our thoughts, feelings, and sensations in the body without getting caught up in our emotional reaction to them. Our minds are always chatting, commenting, and evaluating. Let's see if we can understand a bit more about what happens for you.

Try it now 1
Take a moment to consider this scenario.

It's a bank holiday and you have found yourself at the start of a fun run with friends. You would of course be up for this if you hadn't spent the night before eating too much rich food, and now was nursing a slightly churned stomach. You're tempted to walk away but the friends around you assure you it's all just for fun and there will be food and relaxing after. Reluctantly you get started. Soon all your friends have sped off into the distance and you find yourself at the back struggling to get into a rhythm. (Check in

---

with your thoughts, feelings, body right now as you think about this scenario, what's going on for you. Any urges to respond coming to mind?)

As you continue the run you start to get a little more rhythm but realise your tummy is not feeling great. You slow down and get overtaken by a runner pushing a buggy with a child in it. A few moments later you are overtaken by a fun runner in a bear costume. (Check in with your thoughts, feelings, body right now as you think about this scenario, what's going on for you. Any urges to respond coming to mind.)

As you turn a corner you realise you are halfway, the route laps back and you start to see people who are about to finish coming in your direction, they look fresh and full of energy. Another corner and you notice you are at the bottom of a steep hill (Check in with yourself. What's in your thoughts now, what are your emotions doing, what does your body feel like? Any urges?)

Take a moment to notice how this felt for you. Notice the minds chatter, what did it say? Was it helpful, unhelpful, or neutral? Would any of this get in the way of your enjoyment or performance. What would it have been like if you were able to move away from the power of these experiences, to put space between you and the natural chain of thoughts and feelings that occurs?

Mindfulness gives us a chance to put a little space between us and the chatter. To separate ourselves from the thoughts, feelings and urges that occur when we are struggling or challenged. It allows us the space to choose how to respond. For some of us the above scenario would create all sorts of negative thoughts and urges to quit. Believe it or not, that's not a problem. It's quite normal and makes sense that the mind would want us to let go of something that is difficult and uses all our energy. After all, the mind doesn't know that you won't need that energy later for survival. It's simply trying to protect us. The thought itself need not be a problem. What makes a thought difficult is when we then add another thought, and another and another and each one triggers an anxious or overwhelmed feeling. Suddenly we are not having a thought, we are thinking and it's not leading us anywhere helpful. It's difficult to think clearly in that space. We find ourselves flustered and unable to make clear decisions. Most importantly we find our minds take us far from the present moment. They take us into the imagined future, they take us to the worst-case scenario or the past. The thoughts argue and before we know it, we are no longer present in our own bodies. Here is the key question. How can you enjoy life or be at your best if you are not there?

SETTING MINDFULNESS GOALS

When we are involved with sports our goals often take on an achievement focus. We often set a target for distance or speed, such as to run our first 5KM or our debut marathon. These goals are great, they are clear, specific, measurable and we can tell if we have achieved them or not. These kinds of goals give us focus and something to measure as we go about our ambitions. With mindfulness there is no doubt these goals can be helpful, but mindfulness goes beyond this. To set goals which mindfulness can support us with we have to look a little deeper at what is holding us back from achieving these goals. How are our minds or emotions getting involved to hold us back from the progress we hope to make?

Try It Now 2
Take a moment to think back over your experience of running when you have not been at your best. It might help you to go back to the scenario in the last try it now section. Have a look at the notes you wrote. What thoughts and feelings got in the way? What emotions, memories or images were there holding you back? Be honest with yourself, how do you get in your own way? This could be before you run, during the preparation stage, during the event or even afterwards. What do you believe about yourself, your

ability, or your body? What do you need to believe about yourself to be able to get out of your own way? These are the things mindfulness can support you with.

See if you can set yourself some goals now that mindfulness can support with. So rather than a goal of run 5K or run a marathon in a certain time, try to explore what's holding you back from that. Perhaps it's the thoughts that you can't do it, or the difficulty in believing in yourself. Perhaps it is simply getting overwhelmed with the task which feels too big. Turning these difficulties into goals i.e., to practise coming back to the present when the mind goes into a negative prediction state or to use mindfulness to help you get out of bed on cold days or simply to look around you more and notice the environment that is hosting your run.

Once you have an idea of a mindful goal it can be helpful to break it down to a SMART goal. This stands for a goal that is specific, measurable, achievable, realistic and has a time frame attached. This can help you clarify the steps you would need to reach the goal.

For example – A mindful goal may be to work on negative thinking when you are stood at the bottom of a hill. This goal can become SMART by breaking it down.

Specific – How are you going to do this? Example, take yourself to a hill and notice the thoughts that come up. Become aware of their impact on your mind, emotions, urges and body. Use your mindfulness practise to help you put space between you and these thoughts, to recognise them as just thoughts. Get yourself to the top of the hill despite the thoughts.

Measurable – This is a measurable goal as you know when you have achieved it. You will be stood at the top congratulating yourself.

Achievable & Realistic – Check in with your goal. Is it too much right now or is it realistic? Always break the goal down to something that is realistic. It doesn't make sense to have your first running goal as run a marathon next week, when you could work on getting to your first 5K event and build on this.

Time framed – Give yourself a realistic timescale. If you recognise this goal is going to take some time, give yourself that time. Having a SMART goal based on a mindfulness objective will help keep you motivated and accountable to yourself.

LIFE ON AUTOPILOT

Imagine what it would be like to press a button somewhere on our bodies and send them off to our jobs, the school run, the supermarket. Imagine being able to let the flesh get on with the tasks we get bored of, while our minds remain free to relax. A kind of autopilot or cruise control for our lives. Should an emergency occur, we could jolt right back into the body and deal with it but in the meantime, we could let cruise control take care of the day to day. Sound good? What if I said most of us are living that way already?

Example

Consider this example. It's been a long day and you are on your way home from work. As you arrive home you become aware that you must have crossed two roundabouts and a set of traffic lights. Yet when you get home, you really can't remember the journey. You were there, your body was there, yet your mind was jumping from thought to thought. Images of your day, thoughts of tasks you never got to, planning what to have for dinner. The mind never stops. From one thought to another, taking us far away from the present moment experience.

Many of us exist in a state where our mind and body are far from connected. None of this is our fault. Our human minds have given us this wonderful quality of being able to move between living in the past, the present and the future. At every moment we have the option to be aware of our past, the present moment and the imagined future.

Sometimes our minds will go into the past for long periods of time, we may ruminate or go over events of the day, conversations, memories, half-finished projects. We get stuck trying to make sense of it all. These could be unpleasant thoughts and memories, or they could be happy times or even more neutral experiences.

Other times perhaps we are living in the present moment, hearing a child laugh, enjoying a good meal, looking out over a beautiful view. In those moments we may be blissfully unaware of anything else that makes up our life. We aren't thinking about our bills, our pensions or when we get time to do the grocery shopping. We may even be so involved we lose track of time. Remember that timeless feeling of your first kiss or dancing to your favourite song. In those moments we are locked in the present. Fully engaged with the moment.

The present isn't always a happy time. Perhaps we get stuck in what seems like an eternal present in a more difficult way. Unable to move beyond a pain that seems to be affecting our whole being or being in the turmoil of a difficult emotion like sadness. In these moments we often try to push away the present, to deny it being here. We put up a fight, a bit like if we fall into quicksand or deep water, we might panic and throw our arms and legs around, kicking against the water in the hope it will somehow calm.

Other times our minds wander to the imagined future, how we picture things going. Sometimes the mind brings up something realistic, sometimes it's fantasy. It can range from a beautiful daydream to a series of worrying 'what if this happens?' thoughts, creating intense anxiety.

Try It Now 3
Ask yourself the question. How much of today did I spend in the present moment? How much of it was on autopilot, body present, mind elsewhere? How much are you already on cruise control and how much does this mean you miss of life?

Try It Soon 4

What if you ask yourself this question again after a run? How much were you present? How much of you was there in the moment? How much did you miss?

Try It Soon 5

Take yourself off for a run and dedicate 5 minutes of that run to simply focussing on the running and noticing every time your mind wanders? How many different thoughts come up in that time? How busy was your mind? Where did you notice the mind wandering to?

MYTHS ABOUT MINDFULNESS

As we start to practise mindfulness or any skill our mind will try to make sense of it. The way the mind does that is by holding onto anything it knows of that is somehow similar. Imagine a new creature is discovered in the world and we see pictures of it for the first time. Our minds may not know what it is, so they fill in the blanks for us. They tell us 'oh it's a bit like a lion, or a tiger but it's paws are like a sloth'. Our minds are filling in the blanks with things we know. This is a helpful tool us humans have developed for when we don't quite know the answer, or something doesn't make perfect sense.

Unfortunately, there is a darker side to this gift. It can make us stuck in ideas that don't quite fit. Imagine we stubbornly said that new animal is a big cat. When evidence of its bone structure or genetics proved, it was related to another species, we may find it difficult to shift our minds, leading us to always refer to them as a big cat.

The same can happen when we carry assumptions or ideas about something which we haven't tried yet. Our minds say it must be like this or must be done this way and that can get in the way of really experiencing something new. With this in mind let's look at some of the common myths of mindfulness which we may be carrying and see if we can let some of them go.

Myth 1 - I need to be religious to practise mindfulness

This is a common myth about mindfulness. The practise we know today has its roots in Buddhist philosophy and therefore plays a role in the lives of many who practise a religion of spirituality. However, it is a practise which has been developed for a wider audience. Although many people with a religious belief meditate and develop their mindful awareness, many meditators have no religion or belief. In fact if we think about the definition of mindfulness which we discussed earlier 'mindfulness refers to the awareness that emerges for us when we learn how to pay attention to the present in a way that is <u>deliberate, on purpose</u> and allows us to simply <u>observe</u> our experience of our thoughts, feelings, and sensations in the body without getting caught up in our emotional reaction to them' we can see that this could be applied to someone with or without any spiritual background or belief.

Myth 2 - I must be sat on the floor with my legs crossed to meditate

There is no doubting the stereotypical image of someone who meditates, as being sat crossed legged on the floor, spine perfectly straight, a calm look upon their face and on each hand the fingers and thumbs joining up to make a perfect circle. It would be easy to feel this is essential for meditation. You wouldn't be too far wrong. This can be a part of mindfulness meditation. Being sat on the floor may aid connection to the earth, while having your spine straight and your posture relaxed but alert can enable us to notice and be with our breath, while providing plenty of space for the breath to travel down the body right into the diaphragm. So, this may be how someone meditates but it is not the only way. Ancient practises like yoga and Tai Chi have shown us how you can practise meditation and develop mindful awareness in a very different way. Here the body is in movement as we bring our full awareness to the present moment.

Let's revisit the definition once more, 'mindfulness refers to the awareness that emerges for us when we learn how to pay attention to the present in a way that is <u>deliberate</u>, <u>on purpose</u> and allows us to simply <u>observe</u> our experience of our thoughts, feelings, and sensations in the body without getting caught up in our emotional reaction to them,'

We can see how this could apply while being sat or while moving. Meditation can take place in several ways. In this book I will introduce you to different ways of meditating. There will be some meditations which involve being seated, laying down, walking, running or even while eating. Meditations can also take place for varying degrees of time. It may be that you practise for a short period of time or that certain practises take you into an in-depth awareness over longer period. The most effective way to learn is to use a combination. Think of the formal meditation as being time to develop a skill and the mindful running as using that skill. Just like when you learn to drive, you may spend hours navigating quiet roads before you feel ready to tackle the busy city centres. These longer meditations provide you with that skill, then you are ready to go ahead and make the most of it while running.

Myth 3 - Meditation is all about emptying my mind

As part of the stereotypical view of meditation is the idea that the successful meditator can empty their mind of all thoughts. This is not actually possible. Our minds like to think, they like to entertain us, to problem solve, to guide us. They are naturally very busy all the time. Our goal in bringing meditation to our lives is not to empty our minds but to notice them. To become aware of them. To move out of the autopilot that many of us live in. It's likely that when we start to meditate on something whether it's the breath or the soles of our feet connecting with the floor as we run, our minds will get involved. They will bring up thoughts, feelings, images. Perhaps these will relate to the experience of running, but just as likely the thoughts will be random and unconnected. Our task is not to banish this mind wandering but to become aware of it. As we become aware of it, we allow ourselves the chance to respond how we feel would be helpful rather than straight out of the autopilot.

Imagine you had a headache. There are ways you could respond to that headache which are skilful. It may be a good idea to drink some more water, to remove yourself from loud environments or to take a rest. To respond skilfully to the headache, you first need to recognise and accept that it is true you have a headache. That frees you up to think how to respond. By acknowledging it you are not saying, it's ok I have a headache you are simply noticing it's presence. Our thoughts, feelings, sensations, and images are like this. If we ignore them or push them away, they rarely stay quiet, in fact they often come back stronger. When we notice and realise, they are there we have a chance to respond in a way that feels right for us.

Have a look at the chain reactions below which occur when we get caught up with difficult thoughts, feelings, or sensations. See if you can notice any reactions, you have that might be unhelpful while running, preparing for a run or even after an event. Consider how you would respond automatically versus if your mind had the space to consider a skilful response?

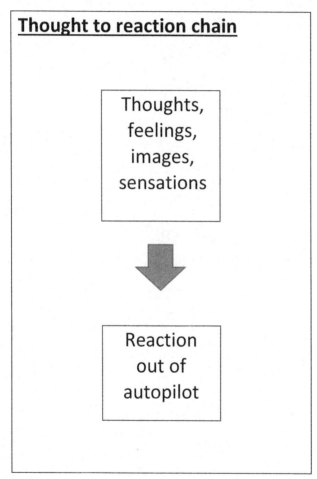

<u>Thought to reaction chain</u>

Thoughts,
feelings,
images,
sensations

Reaction
out of
autopilot

Thought to reaction chain with mindful awareness

Thoughts,
feelings,
images,
sensations

MINDFUL AWARENESS

CHOICE

Skilful
response

WHERE DID ALL THIS MINDFULNESS STUFF COME FROM?

The origins of mindfulness date back thousands of years to eastern philosophies which place a central importance on the practise of meditation. The kind of mindfulness we tend to know in the western world developed more recently. Jon Kabat Zinn developed a programme of mindfulness for stress reduction in the 1970's. This offered a new kind of treatment for Americans suffering with chronic pain or health conditions which modern medicine was unable to help. At the time it was experimental. Later, research suggested it could be extremely helpful for several concerns including preventing relapse into depression and developing acceptance of unchangeable situations. We began to realise the power mindfulness could have to support us in everyday life.

Mindfulness particularly aimed at people in sports began with Jon Kabat Zinn's study into the impact of mindfulness training for elite rowers. It suggested mindfulness had a promising role to play at helping the athletes develop five key skills which would help them perform at their best as individuals and a team. The five key skills can be found in chapter three. Further research followed, resulting in the development of several programmes of mindfulness aimed at athletes. This included the development of Mindful Sports Performance Enhancement (MSPE) created and popularised by psychologists Keith Kaufman, Carol Glass and Timothy Pineau, which was based on the original work of Jon Kabat Zinn.

As we practise mindfulness there are a few qualities to keep in mind. These will help you to observe the present moment with a non-judgemental stance. Don't worry if you don't feel these are strong for you yet. The process of practicing mindfulness will help them to develop and grow within you. Take a moment to consider how each one may be beneficial to you both as a runner and as a person navigating life.

Qualities Of Mindful awareness
Acceptance
Non-judging
Patience
Beginner's mind
Letting go
Trust
Non striving

Many of these can be summed up with the quality of curiosity. If you approach the experience with a sense of curiosity it will in turn help you tune in and notice the present in the non-judgemental way of mindfulness.

CHAPTER 3

HOW CAN MINDFULNESS SUPPORT MY RUNNING?

Regular meditation practise can support us to develop our mindful awareness and our acceptance of our present moment experience. An increase in awareness and acceptance is proposed to help us develop five skills which are relevant for running. These include the following.

Concentration: A greater ability to concentrate on the run. Imagine how much more present you would be with greater concentration both on your run and in life. When you can concentrate you are less likely to get stuck in unhelpful thought patterns. You are likely to be able to visualise what you want to achieve clearly and move towards it. A deep concentration can lead to a feeling of being so focussed nothing can distract you. It could also allow you to notice things like posture much quicker, particularly when fatigued. In turn this may lead to improved posture, performance, and less injuries.

Letting go: This refers to the ability to let go of things which are unhelpful to us in order that we can focus on what moves us forward. Our human brains are designed to problem solve. It's how we developed tools and learned survival skills. Without problem solving the modern-day world would have missed out on its ability to develop space travel and find new ways to cure cancers. We need this problem-solving ability. Unfortunately, our minds often don't realise when problem solving is either inappropriate because the problem hasn't happened yet or is moving into unhelpful over thinking. Consider the fun run example from earlier. There were lots of opportunities for the mind to get caught up in thoughts that would be unhelpful. Thoughts of the people that overtook you, of being at the back, of not feeling your best. In a competition setting, it's not unusual for the mind to get caught up in the race that others are running and for you to deviate from your plan out of pressure. Imagine if you were able to let go of the unhelpful thoughts earlier, so you could simply focus on each step. Our minds would be free to focus solely on the art of running.

Relaxation in the body: Mindfulness allows us to bring our mind and body back together. We often live our lives as though we are outside of our bodily experience. This is why body language is such a give away as to how we are feeling. We naturally tense our bodies when we are anxious, angry, or stressed out. When we run, we can either run with a relaxed body or a tense body. As we tense up our shoulders become hunched, our back often bends and we lose form. This could mean a greater chance of injuries, trips or falls. As we practise meditation, we become more aware of our bodies. This allows us to notice the tension developing, to recognise the spots on our bodies where we tend to store that tension and to learn how to move the body from tension to a more relaxed position when needed.

Harmony & Rhythm: When we run at our best there is a sense of rhythm between us and our movements. A harmony between what our mind is saying and what our bodies are doing. A rhythm to our steps that allows us to glide along almost as though we are floating. Our breath falls into a rhythm that lets us refill our blood stream with fresh oxygen for maximum performance and comfort. For those of us who love cross country, consider the importance of connecting with the earth, of feeling in touch with what's beneath your feet. Over uneven ground, mud or grass, a sense of harmony with the earth allows for a smoother run.

Forming key associations: Associations between our experiences, thoughts and feelings happen naturally. Imagine you are wandering around a supermarket and a song comes on that you haven't heard since the days of your first love. It can be years later, yet the song can recreate the feeling of being excited, of being in love. It acts as a sort of portal, connecting you with long forgotten feelings.

In running we can easily create negative associations from difficult experiences. Perhaps we had a nasty fall at a certain mile marker or had to drop out of an event early. These can create negative feelings that remain present the next time we pass that mile marker or enter that event again. Many runners talk of certain points in events where they suffer a kind of emotional block. Finding it hard to approach the moment in a positive way. Perhaps it's a certain mile marker or a place in a course where you see runners who are close to the finish while you still have a long way to go. Through mindfulness we can gain a better awareness of the impact of these moments and turn them into opportunities to remind ourselves to come back to mindfulness. To drop into the body or come to a particular anchor, to move us away from the cycle that leads us to feel negative.

These skills are important for developing an ability to regulate our own attention and emotions which are central elements of the experience of being in that almost mythical state of flow.

FLOW

The term 'flow state' was coined by psychologist Mihaly Csikszentmihalyi. It refers to a state where an individual is totally engrossed in an activity. A moment of complete concentration on the task. A moment where nothing else matters. An effortless experience in which the individual may feel almost as though they are not there. Perhaps those moments where running feels so effortless, it's like your legs are moving all on their own. The focus is so strong that the person loses all sense of rumination or distraction. In these moments time can take on a new quality, it may feel time has melted away, has sped up or slowed down around us.

A flow state can be achieved during any activity. Many musicians report this feeling during a performance. It happens for many when dancing or creating art or loosing themselves in a piece of music. For runners, finding a sense of flow can be a powerful experience. Imagine how it would feel to appear to be floating your way up the hill or over the finish line.

WHAT CONDITIONS ARE NEEDED FOR FLOW?

You can't force yourself to be in flow. It's a natural state that can occur when conditions are right but also may not. Not every performance by a passionate and talented pianist will create the euphoric feeling, yet at times it may appear, almost as though it's out of nowhere. Some people experience it regularly, others less so. There may be many reasons for this, like the volume of internal chatter in your mind. However, there are things which can increase the chances of us experiencing flow when running.

The first condition would be that you need to be able to concentrate on the running. The world is full of distractions. There are internal distractions like the never-ending narrative of the mind regardless of whether that chatter is positive, negative, or neutral. There are external distractions, some examples may be our phones, which buzz at us with notifications, or our smart watches that want to tell us our current heart rate or our constant clock watching during an event. To reach flow we need the skills to go beyond these distractions.

Developing the five key skills above can be helpful in facilitating flow. Mindfulness is in many ways a concentration exercise. It allows us to practise being with the present, while noticing the distractions without getting hooked into them. To support this, developing the skills of 'letting go,' of being able to reach 'relaxation in your body' as you run and finding a sense of 'harmony and rhythm' with your movement, could all contribute towards a flow state. Likewise developing an ability to watch your mind, to notice habitual patterns of thought can help you to choose how to respond, paving the way for flow.

Mihaly Csikszentmihalyi highlights that flow state also requires a balance of challenge and capability. A perfect mix of a challenging task and the confidence that you are capable and the task possible.

As you can see there is a lot involved with flow. The run would need to be challenging, your body needs to be working, while at the same time it is essential that you feel ready for it. It's important you feel the training was sufficient and that you are capable of the task ahead while also not feeling it is too easy for you. This really highlights the importance of bringing both physical training and mental training like mindfulness to running. Together they can play a much more effective role than a sole focus on the mind or body.

CHAPTER 4

GETTING STARTED WITH MINDFULNESS – THE BODY & BREATH

Hopefully by now you are getting a good sense of what mindfulness is and how it may support you. The best way to learn mindfulness meditation is to get started with some practise. Learning through experience allows you the chance to come up close to your mind and observe whatever it brings up.

MINDFULNESS AND DIAPHRAGMATIC BREATHING

Let's start with applying the definition of mindfulness to something that has been with us since the day we were born and is always with us, our breath. Most of the time we go through life blissfully unaware of our breath. We carry on eating, sleeping, running and all our daily tasks without giving our breath a second thought. Look more carefully and you will see that the breath can have a lot going on within it, sometimes it's fast, sometimes is slow, sometimes it gets interrupted by a cough or sneeze or even the hard but enjoyable work of running. It also changes over time. As babies we breathe right down into our bellies, in a similar way to when we sing or play an instrument. Gradually many of us seem to move away from the belly breathing and start to breath shallower. When we get anxious, we hold our breath (often without realising) or we breath so shallow that we don't fully take the breath in.

Our breath can be remarkable. It can renew and refresh us while acting as an anchor back to the present moment through the body. It is an anchor back to the body when our minds take our awareness away on the thought stream.

In mindfulness practise, how we breathe is not so important as it is simply to notice the breath.

Try It Now 6
Take a moment sat, standing, or laying down. If it feels safe to do so, then close your eyes. Tune into your breath. Start by noticing where you breathe from, perhaps it's the gateway of the nose or the throat. See if you can drop all your attention and awareness into that place. What do you notice, what is it like? Perhaps it is warm or cold, perhaps the in and out are different in temperature. Just simply become aware of your breath.

Let your attention expand from the place where the breath enters your body and see if you can track it all the way through your body. Notice all the muscles which engage to allow you to breathe. Notice the movement of your body, sensations on the surface of your breath or deep within your body. Notice anything there is to be noticed.

It's not unusual during these moments for your mind to wander or to narrate what's happening. Perhaps the mind asks questions 'what am I doing?' 'I don't have time for this', or maybe it drifts to things you need to do, memories of things that have already happened or simply entertains you with fantasy. If this happens, simply notice where the mind has gone and when you feel ready return you attention calmly to the breath. If you need to do that lots of times, it's not a problem or a sign that you are doing anything wrong. It is simply you are coming out of the autopilot and is worthy of a congratulations or a shiny medal!

Having noticed the breath, we get a chance to decide if the way we are breathing is helpful to us. As runners there are benefits to breathing deeply, right down into the diaphragm. It has the quality of allowing the body to relax, calming physiological stressors, and allowing us to make the most of the breath that we take into our body.

Try It Now 7

Take a moment to tune in and become aware of your breath.

Place one hand on your belly and see if you can feel the rise and fall of your hand as your belly takes in the fresh breath. See if you can breathe deeply into your belly rather than stopping at the chest.

Try placing both hands on your belly with your fingers very loosely linked so your hands are hugging your belly. As you breathe see if you can feel a slight stretch in your fingers and hands as the belly rises, starting to part your fingers.

You may want to experiment with breathing in through your nose and out through your mouth. For a deeper relaxation, try breathing out for slightly longer than you breathe in for. For example, breathe in for a count of 4 and out for a count of 6.

The breath can act as an anchor back to the present. It can be there for us to hook onto when the mind is becoming unhelpful. Noticing your breath will give you the space to choose how you want to continue to breathe.

The rest of the body can also act as an anchor back to the present moment. Once we connect with it, we can also use it to help us make any changes that would support our running, like changing your form so you can breathe better or avoid injury.

THE BODY SCAN

To develop the skill of noticing, stabilising our attention and moving it from one place to another when we choose, we can practise getting in touch the body. The body scan is a meditation which can help us to reconnect with the body, become aware of what is there without judging it so we can choose how to respond to it with skilful action.

Like any skill we start by trying it while we are not under pressure. Gradually as we make the process of scanning our body into a habit, we can move it to scanning while in movement.

Try It Now 8
Get yourself comfortable, ideally laying on your back on the floor, a mat, or a bed. If it feels comfortable for you then place your arms alongside but not touching the body, your palms open to the ceiling if that feels right for you.

Slowly we will go through each area of the body bringing your full focus and attention to that area. Imagine your breath could travel down your body, helping you carry your attention right into these areas.

Toes, tune into your feet. See what you can notice about them, perhaps they are warm, cold, tingling or simply register a blank if that is your experience when you tune into this area.

Ankles, lower legs and knees, what can you notice here. It may be sensations on the surface of the skin, connection with the bed or whatever is supporting you or it could be sensations deep inside, the bones, the muscles, tendons. Don't forget if your mind wanders, your task is not to get stressed or angry but simply to notice where the mind went and when you are ready return your attention to gently scanning the body.

Upper legs – thighs, hips, buttocks. What can you notice here? Any sensations in the body or simply noticing a blank or numbness.

Back – Starting with the lower back and moving gradually up to the centre and the upper part of your back. Simply becoming aware of what is here to be noticed. You may also notice if the mind gets involved, judging 'I like this area, dislike this area' if it happens simply notice where the mind went and return attention to the body when you are ready.

Core – Starting with the abdomen. What is here to be noticed, perhaps tingling sensations, or the movement of your breath. When you're ready, letting your attention travel up the core to your solar plexus and chest. Getting in touch with whatever is here right now. Not judging what is here, simply noticing it's presence. Perhaps even getting in touch with the heart as it beats, keeping us alive.

Hands – Moving your attention to the hands, what can you notice here? Letting the attention move up your wrists, lower arms, upper arms, shoulders until you are holding the whole of your arms from fingertips to shoulder blades in awareness.

Neck and throat – What can you notice here. Getting in touch with what it's like to feel the breath here or swallow.

Face and head – Going through each area of your face and bringing awareness to it. The chin, cheeks, lips, tongue, teeth, ears, forehead and nose. Imagine you could breathe right into you head like a balloon, that you could fill it with fresh breath, refreshing and renewing the face from behind the skin.

To end bring your attention back to the whole of your body, laying here, breathing. Take several mindful breaths and congratulate yourself for taking the time to get to know and explore your body and the minds wandering in this way.

CHAPTER 5

MINDFULNESS WHILE RUNNING

So here we are, aware of what mindfulness is, how it may support us as runners and starting to introduce mindfulness to the process of breathing. The next step is to start incorporating our mindfulness skills while we are moving or preparing for movement. Let's get started on the first part of the definition of mindfulness which is all about paying attention to the present moment. This is directly building on the skills developed while practicing the body scan.

The human mind is a busy place. As we have seen it likes to move between thoughts, feelings, and images, sometimes taking us to thoughts of the future, the past or simply entertaining us. All this means we are having a constant stream of thoughts that rarely takes a break. It's difficult to be in the present when the mind keeps taking us off on streams of consciousness. It's not a problem that the mind wanders, or a sign that you are doing anything wrong. All it says is that your mind is busy being human, its analysing, working things out, making sense of the world. Sometimes, the well-meaning mind can take us far from our present experience and mean we miss important cues that would tell us more about our bodies, make skilful choices in how we cope with our bodies or simply make it difficult to enjoy the experience. In these moments we might need a little help. We need a guide who says to us, come back to the present and here is how you do it. These are often referred to as anchors. Something in the present moment which can anchor us, stabilise us and stop us drifting off.

FINDING YOUR RUNNING ANCHORS

Consider the role of an anchor on a ship. The anchor is responsible for steadying the boat, for keeping it in one place, for being the strength against the tide that wants to carry the ship far away. Once the anchor is down the crew can rest. Our anchors allow us to feel stable within the present. They allow us to bring our attention to the present. When we find an anchor to the present, we place our energy into staying in the present rather than drifting on autopilot amongst our thoughts, images, and emotions. Just like with the anchor in the ocean, the anchor has not calmed the sea, the water continues around it. It continues to remain still amongst the chaos of the tide rather than fighting the tide. When we find our anchors, we are doing the same. We are placing our energy into the anchor rather than trying to argue with the ocean of thoughts and feelings that come up for us. So, let's be clear, when we find an anchor to the present, we can use it to stabilise us in the present, but we aren't banishing or getting rid of thoughts or feelings. Our thoughts will arise whether we give them permission to or not. That is just what thoughts do. Instead, we will learn over time how to observe the thoughts without us having to get caught up in them.

When we practise mindfulness meditation the most common anchor used is the breath. There are some reasons for this. Firstly, the breath is our life force, yet as we grow older many of us change the way we breathe to match a lifetime of stress and anxiety. We move from our natural state of belly or diaphragmatic breathing to breathing from our chest. A shallower quick breath that never quite allows for a full cleansing of breath. Learning to breathe well will help our bodies to relax, to move from a state of fight flight which is a constant state of mild anxiety to activating our bodies relaxed system. This can be helpful when running as it will allow us to notice our bodies tensions and make a choice as to how we would like to respond to these in a skilful way.

Another reason to be with the breath is that the breath will always be with us. It is here for us to anchor ourselves to from birth to death. We will always be able to locate it. Learning to be with the breath can provide us with a lifetime anchor to come back to.

However, it is not the only anchor. We can anchor ourselves to anything in the present. Let's start with the five senses. These can provide us with signs as to what might be a helpful anchor back to the present for us. We are all individual and something that works well for you may not suit someone else. It's a great chance for us to personalise our mindful skills just for us.

Taste – This can provide something to tune into. When was the last time you really tasted that water, that smoothie or energy drink. The great thing about using taste is that throughout a run its likely to change, which can be stimulating for the meditator with an active mind. It's likely to alter as you take on liquids, as you become sweaty, or your mouth become dry.

Try It Now 9

Take a moment to simply sit and be with the sense of your mouth, what can you taste right now? Perhaps there is still a taste of your last meal or the morning coffee is lingering. Perhaps the mouth has a taste of its own in between the stimulation of food and liquids? What is true for you in this moment?

Try It Later 10

Here's a great excuse for you to stop for a moment. Take a seat and settle down with a beverage of your choice, something warm and with flavour like a tea or coffee is ideal. See if you can become truly aware of yourself drinking the beverage. Slow the process right down and see what you can notice. The raising of your hand to your mouth. The touch of your fingers on the cup. The first moment it touches your lips. Don't be in a rush to swallow, simply notice the urge to do so as you hold the drink in your mouth. Notice what the tongue is doing, notice it against the teeth, the back of the throat the cheeks. Simply be with the drink. Continue the awareness as you swallow. Notice the movement of the drink in the throat as it trickles down.

Try It later 11
As you go for a walk or a run, take a drink with you. Whether you like to drink a full bottle with each 5km or prefer a few sips doesn't matter. Each provides you with the chance to practise tasting the liquid as it enters your body. Notice where your thoughts were before the drink, notice how your mind allows you to return your full attention to the present and the taste of the drink when it feels right for you.

Smell – This can also provide a wealth of different experiences. As we rely on our strongest senses first, we often miss others. Smell can be one of those things that we barely notice unless it is pleasant or unpleasant in which case our minds and bodies try to either hold on to the experience or push it away. Opening your awareness to the sense of smell as you run can also open your eyes to really noticing the experience in a way that would have simply passed us by.

Sight – Tuning into what we can see. Humans are great at seeing without seeing. Sometimes we look at things all day long and rarely notice them. If I was to ask you right now to draw a picture of something you see every day like the screen of your computer or the apps that are on your phone screen, without taking a sneaky look. Many of us would struggle to do this accurately. We check our phones many times a day, but we rarely actually see them. We are simply looking for something specific like that new message, that invite to the party or the email that's going to bring our mood down or lift it right up.

Try It Later 12

While out for a run or a walk set an alarm on your phone or make a mental note to spend just one minute of the journey aware of what you can see. Use this time to tune into the shapes, the colours, things close, further away. Don't forget that while doing this, we also need to be aware of our safety and look out for obstacles that might cause a fall.

Try It Several Times 13
Here's a challenge. Try the above activity over several runs or walks. Try going on the same walk and seeing if every time during the 1 minute of observation you can notice one thing that is different in the same location. It doesn't have to be a big change, something as small as that flower I noticed yesterday has been blown slightly different by the wind or the ducks in the pond that were asleep yesterday are now swimming.

Sound – Our modern world is a bombardment of different sounds. From the natural sounds of the birds calling to each other, to the buses, the cars to the ever-present chatter of people. With such a constant stimulation it's not surprising many of us choose to tune it out with earphones blaring the tracks that inspire us or the latest podcasts. The difficulty with this is it can lead to us becoming dependant on blocking out our run rather than being with the run. Sounds in the natural environment can act an anchor back to the present moment, allowing us to really be present.

Touch – The sense of touch can be a powerful and vivid anchor back to the present moment. The body is full of nerves that allow us to feel touch all over. As we run there are endless opportunities to tune into touch. The feet may be your first stop, take your attention to the feet as you run. See if you can notice what each toe feels like, the impact of the ground through your shoes, sensations in the skin but also the bones, joints, cartilage. Perhaps you feel warmth, or moisture or tingling. Notice the sole of the foot on the ground, yet also the sole of the foot as it moves through the air. As we break down the sense of touch in feet we can see how many points of contact there may be, lots of opportunities for anchoring ourselves back to the present. As we move up our body, we can see it's not just our feet. Our ankles may be touching our socks, or touching the air as we move through it, perhaps it feels the wind, the water from puddles, the grass or mud. Each area of our body may have the potential of being a touch point to tune into. The hands and wrists may have a sense of touch when we wear gloves, a ring, or a running watch. Perhaps we can even tune into our fingers touching other fingers. Perhaps we can tune into our sense of touch as we hold a water bottle, how are we holding it? What muscles and bones are involved in the grip? Are they tense or relaxed?

Some Specific Anchors To The Present For Runners

Feet – Connect with the feeling of the foot, the touch of your footwear on your skin, the sound or feeling of the connection with the ground as you land or the emptiness of the foot as it rises to the air.

Hands – Tune into the feelings in your hands, this could be about the movement, the tingling in fingers, the sweat on your skin.

Core – What can you notice here, become aware of muscles, bones, tendons, organs, the feeling of your heart beating, the breath as it moves in your belly or enters and leaves your body.

Legs – You may notice certain parts of the legs like the feeling of calf muscles tensing or

---

the sense of strength in your thighs as you tackle that hill section.

Colours – See what you can notice. Take a moment to come out of autopilot or to move your mind away from thoughts back into the experience of sight. Notice the subtle differences between colours, perhaps the trees have many shades of leaf that our mind may see as one colour until we really pay attention.

Feeling of clothes on skin – You may choose one item that's touching your skin to tune into, or to gently scan your body, tuning into the sense of touch.

Checking in with running posture – Take a moment to tune into your posture from head to toe. What is your body doing? How are your shoulders? How is your back? Are you starting to slouch? At first simply observe where you are now, then allow this knowledge to inform any changes you would like to make.

The wind on your skin – The weather can be a great anchor back to your body. Whether its warm air that is barely moving or blustery winter winds. Tune into where you can feel it, perhaps on your face and hands. Enjoy the feeling. You are very much alive.

The feeling of rain on your skin – What better way to learn to love the wet runs. See if you can feel each splash on your skin, the temperature, how it impacts your skin, feel it run down your body.

Gentle body scan – Once you have practised the body scan you will become familiar with bringing your attention to the whole of the body, starting with the feet and working your way up. Tune into your body. Notice what is here in each area.

Try It Later 14
Muddy Mindfulness otherwise known as mudfulness. This is all about the joy of running through mud and puddles. It's a great chance to feel free. It can allow you to feel the joy you may have felt as a child when you ran simply for the pleasure of running. It's also a great chance to get up close to nature. Take yourself off to the muddiest, wettest part of the park or field and simply run mindfully through it. Bring your full attention to each splash, feel the mud or water as it connects

with your ankles. Listen out for the sound of yourself running through the mud. Notice any thoughts that get in the way like thoughts of having to clean up your running kit after, then you can make a choice to keep running through mud anyway or to follow the thoughts. Muddy mindfulness can give you a reason to love the wet and muddy seasons.

TAKING MINDFULNESS OUT FOR A WALK

Mindful walking is the ability to bring mindfulness to the mechanisms of walking. Don't forget that mindfulness is about the awareness that emerges when we pay attention to the present, without judgement. It's about bringing a curiosity to the experience of walking.

Try It Now 15
Find a small space in your home or wherever you are. Just enough space for a few steps will be enough. We are going to take some mindful walking steps.

Start by standing with your feet roughly hip width apart if this is comfortable for you. You may wish to do this barefoot to help your really connect to your feet. Mindfulness is not an opportunity to relax and go to sleep (though that often comes as a side effect) it is more an opportunity to fall awake. To become aware of what's here and what's happening. So, let's find a stance that represents being awake while also having a relaxed not tense body. With our spine straight and head balanced. Make sure your knees aren't locked, keep some buoyancy and relaxation in muscles and bones. This is a mountain pose, relaxed and strong.

While here, close your eyes for a moment and see if you can let your attention wander down your body to the soles of your feet on the floor. Tune into each toe, to the four corners of your feet, to the curve of your feet. Notice the points of contact, perhaps some areas of foot feel flatter with more pressure than others. Tune into your ankles, the calves, thighs and core, letting your awareness spread all the way up your body.

Slowly we are going to take a single step. Start by gently shifting your weight to the foot that will support you and with patience allowing one foot to rise to the air. Notice all the bones and muscles that are involved. The emptying of pressure on one side, the extra pressure on the other foot. Notice the hips, things and all that is involved as you take the step. Notice the landing on the floor in front of you. Become aware of the movement of your hip and all muscles that are involved as you slowly take a second step.

Continue to take steps. If you need to turn, see if you can become aware of all that is involved with the turn. All muscles, bones, cartilage, tendons.

You may also notice the mind getting involved. Perhaps it questions what you are doing. Perhaps it comments on the process or brings in emotion like frustration at going so slowly. Let all of this be held in awareness as a part of your experience. You are mindful walking. You are becoming aware of what emerges when you pay attention to your present experience (in your body, thoughts, and emotions) in a non-judgemental way. Here we are bringing curiosity, rather than judgement to our experience of simply walking.

Try It Later 16

Take mindful walking outside. This time with shoes on unless you are lucky enough to have an area where you won't get hurt like a soft sand beach. Tune into all that that you did at home.

-The feet, bones, muscles, cartilage, sensations on the skin and deep within

-Scanning the body, noticing all that is here as we walk.

-Noticing times when the mind chooses to comment, without getting caught up in those thoughts. If you find yourself getting lost in thoughts simply bring yourself back to the anchor of your feet on the ground.

-Play around with curiosity. Let this be fun. Slow down your walk, speed it up, sometimes have long strides, sometimes short, all the time seeing what you notice, becoming aware.

-Take a moment on each of the five senses, tune into touch, taste, smell, sound, sight. See what you can notice.

-Try revisiting the section on anchors. For a few minutes choose a particular anchor and see what it is like to bring your attention here.

BUILDING TO A RUN

By now you will be getting a sense of what mindfulness is and how you can be mindful during movement. It's time to get out for a run in a mindful way. So, what do we need to remember to run mindfully? Mindfulness is all about being with the present moment in a non-judgemental way. The way we do this is to anchor to something in the present moment which can help keep us focussed on the here and now. Let's get started.

Try It Now 17
A mindful preparation for running could include the following.
Mindful hydration – The process of being mindful starts way before the run. See if you can hydrate and refuel in a mindful way. Bring your full attention to the liquids or foods you consume in preparation. Perhaps having breakfast or a snack in a mindful way.

Bring your full attention to the food or drink. Smell it and see what you can notice? Taste it slowly. Bring it first to your lips, then let it move to your tongue. Slow the process of eating and drinking right down. Let things linger on your tongue, simply noticing the urge to chew, to swallow or move on quickly. Allow yourself to fully taste, to experience things sliding down your throat. See if you can really notice the hydration.

Try It Later 18
When you are ready for a run you can take the opportunity to dress in a mindful way. In particular, the lacing up of running shoes. This may be something we would usually do very quickly in a hurry to get going. Slow the process down. Tune into your fingers as they touch the shoes, sensations in your toes and feet as they receive the footwear. Take your time noticing each movement of your fingers, legs or feet as you do this. Become fully aware of all that is involved in the delicate art of shoelace tying. Bring your sense of curiosity to the process, as though it is the first time you have ever done this task.

Try It Later 19

Mindful warm up. As you prepare for your run bring mindfulness to your warm up. Keep in mind what it was like for you to mindfully move during the walking and see if you can bring similar qualities to the warm up. However you usually warm up, whether this is a set routine of movement like back kicks, circling arms, gentle jogging or simply a walk that gradually build to a run, the important thing is to bring your awareness to it. It may help to choose a single anchor you would like use throughout, like noticing the sensations in the soles of your feet. Whatever warm up exercise you are doing you could tune into this and simply notice what is here. Alternatively, you may choose to bring the awareness to the whole of your body by moving it around (just like we did in the body scan) depending on what exercise you are doing at the time. The important thing is that you bring awareness to the movement, bring a sense of curiosity. Remember, pure curiosity is not judgemental. It won't say you are doing this wrong, but curiosity may notice and observe how the mind gets involved and brings up the thought you are doing something wrong. This is simply a thought. You can choose what to do next.

Try It later 20
Mindful run – it's time to put it all together. To start the process of mindful running. You have lots of choices as to how you would like to do this.

Choice 1 – head out for a run and see if you can become mindful and anchored to the present in short bursts. Concentration is a difficult skill, and it comes up against the minds natural tendency to wander, think and entertain. So, it is unlikely you will be mindful for a whole run. There will be many times when you notice you had been focussed and yet somewhere the mind had decided to take your attention and you find yourself waking up from an autopilot moment where you're not even sure what you were thinking about. If this happens it is not a sign that you are doing anything wrong. Simply that the mind is a busy place. Congratulate yourself on noticing and waking up. In this moment you have become mindful. Then simply bring yourself back to an anchor when you can.

Choice 2 – Set yourself a plan of a minute of mindfulness. See if you can really tune in to an anchor in that time, whether that anchor is your footsteps, the sensations in your ankle, hands or simply the sound around you is less important. Simply tune into whatever is here in this moment. It may help to set a timer that can remind you to start a minute of mindfulness. If after this minute you feel you would like to continue then why not make that the most of it. If it feels like enough then you could congratulate yourself on achieving your goal and perhaps form the resolve to continue with each run to have a minute of mindfulness. Perhaps even choosing to gradually build up this time.

Choice 3 – Set yourself a mindful challenge along your run. Something that will keep you in the moment. Perhaps this could be that every mile marker you do a gentle body scan, observing what's here in your body as you move your awareness from toes to head. Or perhaps it could be to notice how many different shades of green there are on the trees, or simply to notice something about a regular run that you have never noticed before.

Don't forget to warm down and stretch out in a mindful way to. Perhaps there is a particular exercise that you would like to bring your awareness to, or simply see how much of the warm down routine you can observe.

CHAPTER 6

WATCHING THE MIND AS IT WANDERS

The present moment can consist of many things. As we observe the moment we may focus on the breath, an anchor to our senses or even our thoughts. The thoughts which emerge in our mind as we bring our attention to a task can consist of any form, perhaps they are memories, what we need to do later, events that have happened, images or simply the mind recalling our favourite song lyrics. One of the biggest myths about mindfulness is that we must empty our mind of thoughts. It's not actually possible to clear our minds and not experience thoughts. That may be a disappointing realisation when we humans spend much of our time fighting with our thoughts, trying to supress or banish them. Quite often we may respond to a thought that is unhelpful or distressing in some way by distracting ourselves from it, refusing to give it airtime in our minds. When we do this our minds become engaged in a fight. We become tense at the mere presence of the thought and find it even harder to let go of its power. Mindfulness offers us a way of giving up the fight with thoughts. That doesn't mean we give up, start ruminating and become stuck. It simply means that rather than fight the thoughts we step back and observe them before making a more skilful choice of how we would like to respond.

Consider the following example. You are coming back from an injury. As you start to warm up and begin a gentle jog you notice a twinge near the injury sight. Thoughts could go in many directions. The mind may take you to the future and say that this is the injury back and it's going to get worse. Perhaps the mind says give it time, it's just because your muscles are not conditioned. For many of us it may be more of a mix. We often hold positive, negative and neutral thoughts in our mind. Perhaps the thoughts lead to emotions, panic or frustration. The mind remembers the injury, the loss of running, perhaps the weight gain, the mind tells the body this is something to panic about and begins the process of preparing your body to run away or fight by filling it with adrenaline. Your mind begins to run through thoughts. It becomes more difficult to concentrate, to decide as to what is right for you and your body. Mindfulness can support us in recognising this storm of thoughts, separating them out and calming the physiological sensations of stress. All this makes it easier to step back from the situation and make choices based on what you think is right rather than on the emotion or physiological response.

Observing the mind and practicing being with our thoughts rather than instantly reacting to them is a skill that we can develop through practise. Let's get started with simply observing our mind.

> **Try It Now 21**
> **The TV screen meditation** – Settle somewhere comfortable and close your eyes. Take a moment to arrive in the present by tuning onto 3 mindful breaths. When you are ready, use your imagination to picture a TV or cinema screen. Simply focus all your attention on the screen. As you make it the centre of your awareness it's likely the mind will want to comment. If you notice a thought, see if you can put it up on the screen, either as words or an image. You get to take your place in the auditorium and simply observe the thought, without adding to it or rejecting it. After all, it is here anyway, you get to simply acknowledge and observe. Notice as thoughts come and go. Some thoughts staying on the screen a while, others moving on and being replaced by new thoughts quickly.
>
> Some thoughts will be easier to observe than others. Some will feel like they call you into the screen, to add more thoughts to them, to

argue with them or to get in a conversation with them. There may be times you find yourself waking up and noticing that you were caught up in the thought. If this happens it is not a sign that you are doing anything wrong, simply that your mind likes to think. Your task is simply to notice where the mind went, place this thought up on the screen and return to simply observing the thoughts as they come and go.

Try It Later 22
Observing the mind as we run – A fun and intriguing exercise can be to start observing your thoughts as you run. As you run along say your thoughts out loud. So, if your mind comments on the fatigue, say it out loud. If your mind notices a particular bird, say it out loud. If your mind is on food for that day, say it out loud, this all helps us to observe and notice the commentary of our mind as it gets involved without experience of running. We can even then notice the impact these thoughts have on our body and emotions as we run. If you notice lots of thoughts of being

overwhelmed at work, what does this do to your posture, to your curiosity, to your motivation?

VISUALISATION

Mindfulness, the awareness that emerges when we learn to pay attention to the present in a deliberate, non-judgemental way, can be said to sit within a larger world of meditation. Mindfulness is an aspect of meditation which helps us to come back to whatever we are focussing on. Mindfulness is also the product of meditation. As we practise meditation mindful awareness emerges and begins to spread from our meditation time to moments in our daily lives.

There are many types of meditation which come from their own unique traditions. These different meditations may involve a focus on a particular point of attention i.e. the breath or feeling of our feet on the floor. Meditations may also involve using affirmations or mantras, which are about focussing on words that create a feeling. A third type of meditation may involve visualisation. This can be particularly helpful for runners, or even when life throws a difficult situation your way. They can help us in two main ways.

1) To help us visualise and become fully familiar with feelings around our sport. This can be incredibly motivating and can support you before a run to get your mind into the feeling of running with a sense of flow.

2) To develop a sense of how we would respond to thoughts, feelings, sensation in the body that may come up for us during a run. Particularly if these experiences emerge because of unexpected events which could not have been foreseen.

The exercise below can help you get started with visualisation. This script allows you to become familiar with, cultivate, and grow the feeling of being in flow when you run. Every time we practise this, we open ourselves up to the belief that we can run well. We can also use this to build motivation to get us out on those cold, dark winter mornings. To add to the exercise below you may also choose to add in noticing difficult thoughts or feelings, sensations that may arise and considering how you would respond to those in the moment. This can help us to prepare in advance for them, making mindfulness even more familiar and therefore something we are going to be able to use in the presence of difficulty.

Try It Now 23
<u>Getting Started With Visualisation</u>
-Find a comfortable position, sitting or lying and bring your attention to the breath to help you settle.
-Locate a memory of running at your best, in a sense of flow or if this is difficult you can simply imagine running at your best. This works best if you can bring your attention to this image as you would have seen it, through your own eyes rather than watching yourself on a movie screen.
-Tune into your sense of sight within this image. Notice what you can see as you run in

---

flow, perhaps it's people cheering you on, perhaps it's the course ahead of you or your arms as they work to propel you forwards.

-Tune into anything you can hear as you run in flow. Listen out, what sounds are here, perhaps they are from other runners, sounds in the background, sounds from your own body.

-Notice any sense of taste that might be lingering in your mouth, perhaps your mouth is dry or there are the lingering sips of energy drinks or the freshness of water and you stay hydrated.

-Become aware of any smells, perhaps you are running by the sea or there is the smell of grass or even the aroma from local restaurants.

-Become aware of touch. Tune into your body within the visualisation. Noticing any sense of connection between your body and the surface beneath your feet, perhaps noticing the feeling of your trainers, your clothes on your skin, even the gentle touch or the air, wind or rain on your skin.

-Tune into an overall feeling of how your body feels in this moment. What it's like for you to run in flow.

CHAPTER 7

THE ADVENTURE HAS ONLY JUST BEGUN

Congratulations! Your mindful running adventure has well and truly begun. As we reach the end of new information it can be tempting to put the book down and say to ourselves, I know that now. But don't forget the beginners mind, the concept of coming to everything as though for the first time. This is a great opportunity to practise this attitude as we continue to learn mindfulness. You may remember me saying at the start of the book that it is the mindful practise itself which is likely to be your teacher. I would like to present you with an option of treating this book as a 4-week mindfulness course which will equip you with a framework for developing a longer-term mindfulness practise. It all depends how ready you are. Mindfulness can be an idea that you bring into your life at certain times over a long period of time, with many times where you practise more than others or finding yourself not practicing. However, to really understand mindfulness and develop the skills it can be helpful to have an immersive experience of mindfulness practise. A time where you delve into meditation in a deeper way. Think of it like learning to drive or ride a bike, there may be a time where you must practise regularly. It's hard to pick up a new skill and feel confident with it. If you are learning to ride a bike or drive and you only have a lesson once a month, progress will be slow. If you have more regular lessons for a short period of time you would develop the skills much more quickly and in future this would make it possible to only ride your bike once a month and still have the skill available to you. If you practise mindfulness in an immersive way, then you will be able to make much more use of the mindful runs or the brief moments where you choose to apply it all later.

Week 1 – Finding Motivation & Adding Mindfulness To Your Run

– Read Chapter 1,2,3 & 4.

This week we start to consider how mindfulness could support us and our running. We begin to see what thoughts, emotions, reactions, memories, and judgements we carry with us that may get in the way of our sports performance or enjoyment. We set some mindfulness related goals based on what is getting in the way.

– Complete the TRY IT exercises 1, 2 & 5 from chapter 2. Revisit them in the book for further instruction.

TRY IT exercise 1 – Visualisation. This practise introduces us to a scenario around running that may feel familiar. See if you can notice what gets in the way of you being your best or enjoying your run? Perhaps it's the thoughts, the emotions, the stories we tell ourselves.

TRY IT exercise 2 – Set some mindful goals. These will be SMART goals based on the things you identified as getting in the way of your ability to be present, be at your best performance or enjoying the run.

TRY IT exercise 5 – Take yourself out for a walk or a run. Spend 5 minutes just focussing on the run and noticing when your mind wanders.

Meditation – Noticing your breath for 5 minutes 3 x a week. Use the TRY IT exercises 6 & 7 from chapter 4 to guide you.

Week 2 – Building A Mindful Practise

This week we build the skills of mindfulness. As we practise the body scan meditation, we start to stabilise our attention on one area of the body, then practise moving that attention. Practicing this many times while laying or sitting can help us make this ability more natural. We are then able to use it to guide where we would like our attention to be when we are running or moving or in increasingly stressful situations.

Meditation – TRY IT exercise 8. Body scan practise 10 minutes a day 5 times over the next week. Set aside 10 minutes and gently scan through your body from your toes up to you head. Notice sensations in the surface of your skin, the bones or ligaments, muscles and joints. If the mind wanders, notice with curiosity where it went then gently guide your attention back to the body when you can.

Week 3 – Making Mindfulness An Everyday Practise

This is the week you have been waiting for. Our practise ramps up and takes us outside for a mindful run. Revisit the TRY IT exercises to support you and offer choices of how to approach your final mindful run.

– Read chapter 5

Meditation – TRY IT exercise 10. This meditation involves bringing all your sense to a beverage. Take some time out from your day and see what you can notice.

Active Meditation – TRY IT exercise 16. This meditation involves bringing mindful awareness to the experience of walking.

Active Meditation – TRY IT exercise 18. In this practise we start adding mindfulness to all the preparation involved with a mindful run. We are starting to bring our skills from the body scan into everyday life. In this practise we bring our attention to the act of tying our laces.

Active Meditation – TRY IT exercise 19, let's bring our attention to the process of warming up. As we warm up let's bring the mindful outlook of being with the present moment in a non- judgemental, on purpose way.

Active Meditation – Our first mindful run – revisit TRY IT exercise 20 for detailed instruction and options of how to approach your run.

Week 4 – Deepening Practise – Understanding Our Thoughts

Our final week of the immersive mindful running experience begins right here. By now the idea of mindfulness and the practise of adding it to running may feel familiar. This week we deepen our practise by becoming aware of our thoughts and in particular the unhelpful thinking patterns we may get stuck in.

– Read chapter 6

Meditation – TRY IT exercise 21. TV screen meditation 2 x in the week. In this practise we start to observe our thoughts in the same way we would observe our breath or our anchors back to the present. When we are running this can support us to notice the wanderings of the mind. Over a longer period, this practise can also help us identify the patterns of thought that we continually get caught in. The more able we are to notice them; the more chance we have to respond to them how we feel is right for us, rather than responding out of autopilot. Revisit the exercise for further instruction.

Active Meditation – TRY IT exercise 22. Observing thoughts while running. This offers a chance to take the skill of observing thoughts and choosing how to respond to them outside and apply them during a run.

As we come to an end of the course it's a great chance to reflect and recommit to the practise. Take some time to consider what mindful practises you would like to continue, how frequently and why it is that you want to practise? Having had this immersive experience in mindfulness and mindful running, now is a time to find a plan that you can confidently fit into your life. Perhaps it's to continue the body scan daily, weekly or to stick to mindful practise when you exercise. Whatever your plan, you have already planted the seed of mindful running and now is the opportunity to keep watering it and watch it grow over time.

In this section I will recap the main points from the book. Before reading on, take some time to consider your own learning points and experience. It may help you to consider the following questions.

Reflecting On The Experience

What has been the delights and difficulties of mindful practise?

What beliefs or thoughts about mindfulness did you have before reading the book and practicing that you feel differently about now?

What mindful practises would you like to continue to work on now we have come to the end of the course?

What are your next steps to adding mindfulness to everyday life or to your running?

The whole course summed up in less than 5 minutes! See how much you can remember.

Key Point 1 - The emotional mind and the mindful mind work differently. The emotional mind often leads to us responding without any thought or reflection, often in a negative way as we are overwhelmed by the feeling. The mindful mind allows us to notice an experience, whether that's a thought, feeling, bodily sensation or memory without having to fuse ourselves with it or give it further power. This allows us to respond to it how we want to rather than out of emotion. This allows us to come out of the autopilot so many of us live in. When we do this, we can really be present with our lives.

Key Point 2 - Mindfulness can be defined as the awareness that emerges for us when we learn how to pay attention to the present in a way that is deliberate, on purpose and allows us to simply observe our experience of our thoughts, feelings, and sensations. There are lots of myths about mindfulness including the idea that it is religious or allows us to empty our mind. None of these are true, we can see from the definition above that mindfulness can take place in everyday life with no need for a religious doctrine, that we can choose to meditate actively and that our minds are far from empty.

Key Point 3 - Mindfulness for sports helps us in 5 key areas.

1) Concentration

2) The ability to let go rather than ruminate or get caught up in a negative experience.

3) A deeper sense of relaxation in the body and being able to spot tension.

4) A sense of harmony and rhythm or connection. This could be with our bodies, the earth, a sense of touch.

5) Changing of negative associations into opportunities to practise mindfulness.

Key Point 4 - Mindful awareness can help us develop the conditions needed to enter a sense of flow.

Key Point 5 - We can experience mindfulness while running by allowing ourselves to tune into the present using anchors to help us. Some examples of anchors include but are not limited to the following.

Connecting with the feet, hands, core of the body or legs. Noticing the feeling of clothes on your skin, the wind or the rain. They could also include looking out for and paying attention to the colours around us.

How did that feel? All familiar or are there things you would like to go back to and revisit? If so, that's fine. Mindfulness is something we learn over time. The practise has just begun.

Three Top Tips

Here are my three top tips for making mindful running a regular part of your life.

1) Get started in a way that feels right for you. Perhaps you are ready to follow the plan above and have four weeks of intensive practise. Perhaps you are ready to simply bring awareness to a few minutes of mindful walking or running. Wherever you are is perfect for you.

2) Practise mindfulness regularly. Ideally every day. It doesn't have to be much, perhaps just making a decision to make your hike up the stairs mindful or adding in a minutes mindfulness to your run. If there are times when you are less active due to injury or illness return your attention to the still meditations, like focusing on your breath or a body scan.

3) Join a community of like-minded people. This may involve joining mindfulness communities on social

media or it may involve talking to the other runners around you about mindfulness. You can join Active Mindfulness social media groups. The details of these are available at www.activemindfulness.org.uk. Connecting with others is a great way of building mindfulness into your everyday life. If you run with others why not invite everyone to join in a minute of becoming aware of your steps or to bring full attention to the warm up.

Mindfulness can be an extremely enriching experience for your sport and general life. Make it a lifelong practise which allows you to continually come back to the moment when it feels right for you. Remember, whatever happens, you can start again at any moment just by taking a new and fresh breath.

Enjoy the present!

Printed by Amazon Italia Logistica S.r.l.
Torrazza Piemonte (TO), Italy

40609355R00060